HOW DOES YOUR GARDEN GROW?

CULTIVATING

A LIFE OF ABUNDANCE

BY: BRIDGETT MCGILL

COPYRIGHT PAGE

To: Amanda,

Thanks for your
support. Wishing you
abundant blessings.

Ms. Bridgett

AUTHOR'S NOTE:

This book is for every woman and the garden that is her life. I pray that every reader is touched, healed and directed to find HER personal answer, to the question – How does my garden grow? I pray all that is here is from The Most High God, Yah, Yahweh, Allah, Buddha, the Creator or whatever you identify your Higher Power to be and I pray you will be lead to peace and rest in your garden. We will no longer look in another woman's garden or give everything in our gardens away. We will learn to love and have contentment in the Uniqueness of our special garden – that is our life.

To the Most High God, I ask all the words come from you and your Word be the evidence that you have written this book to your daughters through me so they may have serenity in their garden-souls. I humbly request that every woman who needs to read this book will be blessed and not denied the opportunity to grow, transform and receive revelation. Let us all tend to, mend, rebuild and take care of the gardens you have given to each one of us.

Allah you are truly merciful, Jehovah you have made me your witness, The Great I Am, you are who you say you are.

Ase'

Show me your garden and I'll tell you what you are.

Alfred Austin

TABLE OF CONTENTS

DEDICATION:

This book is dedicated to my daughters, Kwaanza and Kayla. In raising you, the universe has raised me. You have taught me the true value of loving my garden and yours too. It wasn't always easy, but there was definitely purpose, in our process. Thank you my Daughter-Queens, for the value, joy and most of all laughter you have blessed my life with.

There is no question, without you two, I would NOT be the woman I am today. It is my life's greatest accomplishment, blessing and pleasure to have been chosen by the Creator to be your mother.

Love Mama Bea!

x

CHAPTER 1:

THE SPLENDOR OF THE GARDEN

Greetings sisters and welcome to this journey. As we walk through the gardens of my life and yours, we will discover how closely we are intertwined and how much we all have in common in this complex existence called "life".

We will walk through different gardens to learn, examine, till mend and grow our life-gardens to flourishing abundance.

We will have discovery of ourselves, face up to who we REALLY are, learn new truths and dispel old lies. We will literally, dig out and throw away the parts of our pasts that no longer serve us a purpose. We will say "YES" to a bright new future and a life-garden filled with blessings, love healing and purpose. Please join me and let's start walking, digging and pruning.

According to dictionary.com, a garden is a noun; a plot of ground, usually near a house, where flowers, shrubs, vegetables, fruits, or herbs are cultivated.

1

A garden is feminine, beautiful, lovely and special. It provides beauty to the eyes aromas that tickle the nose and healing for the soul. The beautiful fruit of a garden does not happen on its own. It takes cultivating with intention and purpose. Can a woman come to the garden of your life, be blessed and receive healing?

Our life gardens should be filled with plants of encouragement, flowers of inspiration, vines of motivation and ivies of integrity? Our lives should be a blessing, not a curse.

The bible starts and ends with a garden and has over thirty references indicating gardens were important to our brothers and sisters of old. There are spectacular gardens described in great detail, with such beauty that we can only imagine their magnificence. The gardens of Kings Solomon and Xerxes were like no other gardens and they were evidence of their owner's vast wealth; purple linen, marble floors, cedar and almug trees and benches made of gold were common to both Kings.

Events that forever changed the existence of humanity happened in gardens. Our ancient brothers and sisters experienced gardens in everyday life because gardens provided food. (Jer29:5 & 1Kings 21:2), and medicinal herbs and plants. When a garden was destroyed by worms and pestilence, food supplies and diminished profits were the results (Amos 4:9). This caused distress for people because they ate from the ground; there were no fast food restaurants or microwaves.

They relied on the gardens to sustain life. The bible compares people suffering and living a life in shambles to an un-watered unkempt garden (Isaiah 1:3 & Jer 31:12).

Gardens like Golgotha, where the Lord was laid, served as burial grounds (2Kings 21:8 & John 41:42). Escape routes were mapped out through the grounds of many gardens (Jer 39:4) and mentioned as sacred grounds for purification (Isa 66:17).

Our Lord, when in deep anguish before his destined walk to the cross, prayed in the garden of Gethsemane and asked his Father if the pain he was about to suffer could somehow be taken away. Adam and Eve with everything at their fingertips, were not satisfied in the Garden of Eden and they were evicted after their disobedience (Gen 3). In Revelation, the Most High God promises that those who hear the Word and does what it says, will eat from the tree of life, in God's Paradise at the end of their lives. (Rev 2:7).

The idea of our lives reflecting a garden came to me one day as I was sitting and thinking about my life and the early beginnings of my life-garden. As the oldest of four children, my mother raised me to be in charge of and look after my siblings since I could understand what it meant to "be in charge". When she wasn't home, I had full rule of the house. Whatever I said went; there was no discrepancy or talking back. Bridgett said it and that was that. My siblings and I had the "It's us against the world" attitude. We've always had the belief that we are a four people, one unit team and "We all we got!" In the few years before my mother's passing, she started using drugs and our family life took a shift that forced me to take the full matriarchal lead. No, we didn't suffer homelessness or being without food, but the emotional distress took a toll that followed us for many years. All the while, I had to make sure every day was as normal as possible – if there was such a thing. People from our old neighborhood often mention watching me take care of my siblings; it was unbeknown to me that I was ever being watched.

Losing my mother when she was only 45 and I was 27, shifted my leadership role into very high gear.

I stepped into the role of "Mother" without any formal training. I was the big sister that took care of everything. If there were a problem, I fixed it, if there were an uncomfortable situation, I made it smooth and if there were a need for a spokesperson, I became the speaker. I have no regrets of being what I needed to be for my family and thank Yahweh that my mother raised us to understand the true meaning of love for each other.

Year after year, this is who I was, the big sister/mama. Without ever thinking to say "no", I said yes to every need and whim of my brother and sisters.

You need somewhere to stay, ok, come to my house.

She put you out, what is she thinking, like you don't have nowhere to go, you can come to my house tonight!

The owner wants y'all out by Friday, be here Thursday and I'll put my girls in the room with me.

Whatever situation needed to be handled, I handled it. Every situation, from teacher conferences, hospital stays to prison visits, collect calls and commissary. If they needed it, I gave it or made sure there was a way for them to have it. My garden became so full of everyone else's problems that I neglected much of my own. I had a life filled to capacity and I was okay with it. I had become so accustomed to my family needing me, that I became codependent and developed a need to be needed.

Sounds noble hunh? Big sister, who became Mama, stepping up and always being there for her family. It took many years of living in deep pride and codependency to see just how destructive this behavior would become for myself and my daughters.

The initial plan of taking care of my siblings was all good, but I had no idea how this behavior would spill into EVERY area of my life including my former marriage, relationships, jobs and my children. This behavior became a damaging veil that covered my eyes to the garden of MY LIFE.

I started to examine my life and compare it to a garden. I recalled all the times my mindset had been "I'll give you the shirt off my back", thinking it was noble but not realizing, that I then would be cold. I had never stopped to pay attention to the depletion of my own garden, after I had given every single flower away.

I always thought, it's better to give than receive, because no matter what I give, I'll get it back – somewhere, somehow.

I was blinded to the realization that in my giving, I was depleting not only my garden, but my children's fragile gardens as well.

The idea of the Life-Garden became my every thought. I started researching gardens and tools needed to maintain a garden's health. I began to see that like a physical garden, my life too needed to be cultivated, watered, tilled and fertilized. My thinking changed and I came face-to-face with real-life examples of what needed to change in my life garden so that I could grow and flourish. I learned that it was okay to tend my garden and my garden only, to enjoy its beauty and I DID NOT have to give every flower away because someone else expected me to give to them.

I learned that I couldn't allow any and every seed to be planted in my garden, because of the damage it could cause to other flowers or the soil. I had to become mindful of life-gardeners who didn't take care of their own gardens and therefore had no regard for mine.

Many of you may find that your gardens have been different at different times in your life. As you walk through the gardens of these pages, think about your own life garden now. Is it luscious, flourishing and healthy, or does it need work? Does it need to be watered with the Word of God, fertilized with forgiveness, tilled with love or sown with seeds of humility?

How does your garden grow?

Life, with its twists and turns, will create ebbs and flows to our gardens; some we can prevent and others we can't. Just as a farmer checks the seeds before he plants them, you too have to be mindful of the seeds you allow to get planted in your life. What do we allow in our gardens? What are we watching on tv, what are we listening to on the radio? Who are we entertaining in conversations? Would you allow rabbits and field mice to come in and destroy your backyard garden? Didn't grandma put chicken wire around her garden to keep the critters out? Remember our beloved Scarecrow – the ultimate keeper of the gate? If grandma made sure to protect her physical garden, how much more diligent should we be to protect the gardens of our lives?

Every person should not be allowed the privilege of residing in your life. You have to observe people, pay attention to their actions, and listen to their words. Out of the heart the mouth speaks (Matthew 12:34). People who are not spiritually grounded have worldly views of situations that may not line up with your desire to grow in a certain direction, and they can be likened to weeds and bad seeds.

Especially in romantic relationships!

We have to be careful of falling in love with a man's potential. What is he really going to do in his own life garden and what does he add to yours?

Many men have great intentions, but are those intentions meant to bless you? Every man you meet cannot be allowed room in your garden because of the damage it could cause in the long run. Weeds can sink into the soil very subtly, and before you know it, those weeds have inched around the roots of your roses, slowly crept up the stems and choked the life out of once beautiful, healthy flowers. When the blinders fall off and we can see into the reality of our situation, we ask ourselves, "how in the world did I get here". We saw the signs all the time, but chose to ignore them.

We saw the selfishness that kept raising its head in conversations, the pride that kept wagging its tail.

In the end, you remember every situation that should have been red-flagged:

You spend your money freely, lunches dinners, wanting to be the BEST girlfriend ever, but when he gets a special assignment and you ask "can I have a few dollars when you get paid" he says "I have something to do with that money." Ooohhh, so we can spend mine, but not yours", even then you disregarded the sign as "well, he's not working right now, maybe he needs to play catch up." – yeah right.

All men have an agenda, good, bad or ugly; for this reason, your life cannot be a door standing wide open for any and every body to just walk through. When do you actually discover that a person's agenda was to take care of himself and not you, but through you – usually when it's too late! I know I'm preaching and stepping on some toes here, because those toes have been mine, OUCH! Ask a man these questions before you bless him with the gift of sharing your precious space.

> *"what's your purpose for wanting to get to know me?"*
>
> *"why are you calling me?"*
>
> *"why do you want to hang out with me?"*
>
> *"Do you know your life's purpose and are you choosing me because I am in alignment with that purpose?"*

There are only three responses: 1) they don't know their own life's purpose; therefore, they have no clue of why they should be choosing you, 2) they have a purpose concerning themselves, and they need you to bring that purpose to fruition, OR 3) they know their life's purpose and you align with that purpose. We are afraid to ask these questions, because we love the attention. And you know us as women, we don't want to rock the boat, or send the attention away. Instead, we see the red flags and ignore them, because the attention has us all warm and fuzzy.

What about relationships beyond the romantic type? Some women can be catty, nosey, looking for ammunition against us but whatever it is, people have their own agendas for wanting to be in our lives, sometimes it's just pure jealousy. Another woman can want what you have, and the best way for her to get it is to get real up close and personal, all up in your garden.

Start to evaluate how valuable your life-garden is to you. It is precious and should be filled with all good and wise things that came from all that was bad. If you don't see your life-garden as something special right now, keep reading and you will discover that the beauty of your life has been within you all the time.

CHAPTER 2:

WHAT IS THE CONDITION OF YOUR GARDEN RIGHT NOW?

Countless gardens grow throughout the world. Some of them are: botanic, vegetable, Japanese, flower, Rose, Baha'i, Islamic and Spanish, all are gardens that have unique characteristics. When you look at your life-garden, what type of garden do you see, can you identify the unique qualities of your life, your garden?

Is it bountiful and flourishing, or green in some areas with a few brown patches that need tending, because complacency runs your garden? Is it perfect in every way; form un-matched; or will close examination, reveal every single flower to be fake and plastic? Is your life-garden, empty because you've given away every single flower? Is your garden stagnant, because it's filled with flowers of pain and grief that won't grow or die because you're comfortable with letting them grow every year, like perennials, that need no tending or pruning, they just pop up every spring? Do we have plants in our gardens that are serving no purpose, but we haven't yet made the decision to get rid of them? What type of life-garden do you REALLY have?

I love the concept of a life-garden, because it's so real and tangible. You can look at a garden and see a life you've had, you have now or are on your way to if you're not careful.

The Gardens of Pain and Grief

These gardens can paralyze us for years at a time. Pain and grief can keep our gardens from growing and keep us from moving forward in life. We hold on to pain and grief like security blankets. Why, because letting that blanket go means letting go of the pain and grabbing hold to something else –HOPE. Letting that blanket go means we have to find something else to hold on to and that's gonna take work; talking, praying, confronting and challenging ourselves. We won't let go because holding onto the pain and grief is easier and more comfortable. How many women do you know live a destructive life style, because of what happened in their past? Are you this woman who hasn't given herself a victory pat because she's still here? You're alive, right here, right now, you're in the PRESENT, accept the gift. How long are you going to let a dead past hold you captive from its grave? It's simple, take your hand off of it, let go and stand up straight!

Grief is such a powerful emotion, and we all respond differently. I know very well the paralysis of this pain.

"I'm sorry about yo' Mama", said my friend Annie

"What do you mean about my Mama." I asked
"I think you should call the nursing home," she said
in a shaky voice.

My mother had been dead for three days and already in the morgue at a nearby hospital. Who leaves a message telling someone their mother died and transfers her body without having spoken to anyone voice to voice? This was my garden at that moment – shaken and still, more like frozen at that moment. Driving to the nursing home I was numb, I couldn't cry, I wanted to be mad, but I was just in shock.

I sat thinking to myself; My mama died November 5th, the day I learned of her death was November 8th. Her birthday was October 30th. The whole family went to the nursing home with cake and balloons just a few days ago, now she's dead?

My garden, my life-garden came to a complete halt.

"My Mama was doing good, looked like she was getting better. She was taking short walks from the nursing home. She had regained her speech enough to tell the staff at the Vienna stand what she wanted to eat – now she's gone?"

It's funny how your garden can change in the blink of an eye. In the stillness of my garden, there was Jehovah-Jireh, My Provider, comforting me and letting me know that all was well. I entered the hospital. Even as I shed tears now, I can't explain the pain I felt. The attendant did the best he could to pull back the plastic bag and put it under the sheet he covered her with. He rolled down the top of the plastic as best he could from around her head so I could see her whole face and hair. I thanked God for sending just the right person. He stood against the wall and hummed Amazing Grace while I wept for my mother, who I couldn't believe was lying here frozen and lifeless. I don't know how long I stood there, but the attendant never said a word, he kept humming until I turned to him with tears in my eyes and gave him a hug that he knew meant "Thank you".

I thank The Most High for my church family suffering through the pain with me. They understood why I didn't come to church on Mother's Day and knew that messages about a mother's love made me uncomfortable in those first two years. They helped me restore my garden through prayers, listening ears, shoulders to cry on and love. In time my garden was repaired. It would never be the same, because there was a flower that would never grow again, but the spirit of that flower will always be in my heart-garden.

"I miss you Mama"

My brother was incarcerated at the time and mentions every now and then "I still haven't grieved for Mama yet." My middle sister is very private and to this day, I never knew how her garden changed. My baby sister's garden didn't fare so well. She was the youngest of the four of us, and 11 years old when we put our mother in the nursing home. She was 13 when our mother died. Never knowing her father, our mother was all she had. This created a void in her life that sent her spiraling and to this day she is still recovering from the loss. All of our gardens have changed over the years as we live with the life lessons Mama taught us – good and bad.

When grief comes, don't fight it. Let the tears flow, feel the pain of a loss and cry until it hurts, but don't hold it in. Tears are the cleansers of the soul, just like water nourishes our gardens.

Pain, beyond the grief of losing someone to death is just as damaging to a life. The pain of past hurts, abandonment, forms of abuse can cause our gardens to be rotted underneath, but up close these plants and roses look *healthy enough* for us to cope with everyday life. Do you know what that looks like? It's that plant in the far corner of the garden, it grows just enough to be seen, but it never outgrows the other flowers; it doesn't need to. Every day you enter the garden, it's there, glaring at you, not beautiful like the other flowers. It's just green enough to fit in, but there's something about those roots that are poisonous. Above ground we can't see the impact of these roots, but we know something is wrong because all the other flowers are not growing or dying, they are standing still as well.

Why do we hold onto pain and grief when it no longer serves us? Because if we march right up to that grief plant in the corner of the garden, we have to face it. We face it with spade or sheers in hand, or we turn and walk away. The plants of pain or grief do serve us a purpose for a time. We need to grieve for a loved one we've lost, because we have to, we loved them and then they're gone; without grief, we are not being real with ourselves.

Plants of pain serve us for a while, because they remind us that evil does exist, but love and forgiveness can and does conquer evil. Plants of pain remind us that healing is within our reach - if we desire to be healed. The man at

17

the pool of Bethesda was there for 38 years with the plant of "I can't get down in the water fast enough." You really mean to tell me that in all those years, he had not devised a plan to be the first one in the water when it was stirred? And what about you? Is that plant going to taunt you forever, or are you going to make a plan to put some rock salt around it, cover it with lime or get that steel shovel and dig those roots out until you are down to new soil?

It's not easy, especially when that same plant has made us afraid to even come to that part of the garden. We don't want to face who hurt us; we can't find the voice to ever tell them what they did wrong, but the time is now my sisters. We are going into new seasons, with new assignments, and we have to be ready for the new flowers of duty Yahweh wants to plant in our gardens. These assignment-plants cannot be planted in a garden where poisonous roots are waiting to take hold of our destinies and stop our dreams from coming to full bloom. That poison will kill our spirit-plants and stop us from glorifying the Creator.

What do we do when we can't walk right up and start digging? We get gardening sheers and we sit right down next to that poison and snip away, leaf by leaf through confession of the pain. We cut stem by stem, by telling someone how deep the hurt is. We sit with the plant and write a letter. We cry and cry on that plant until our tears start to loosen the dirt around those roots and before long, with spade in hand, that bad boy is coming up and out to be thrown into the fire!

What dreams are being held captive by the pain of your past? Don't you feel the fires of your purpose burning inside you? Every time you read a book, don't you imagine the one you want to write that can change so many lives? Every time you hear a sick child cry, don't you feel yourself comforting them with the words that only a nurse knows? Whenever you witness a child struggling to read, don't the embers of teaching tremble within you? What do you want to do so badly, but the plants of pain and grief won't let you move? Which "lack of faith bush"

needs to be chopped down? How many "daffodils of doubt" need to be uprooted, how many "weeds of fear" need to be snatched out? Can't you feel your gift being stirred every time you're brought face to face with your life's purpose and assignment?

You will make a choice today, with spade in hand. You bend down, dig and dig until the entire root is dug up and thrown into the garbage where it can never take root again, or you walk away with spade in hand, defeated again and let those roots grow deeper.

DO IT grab that mini-shovel, walk right up to that plant, say a prayer and STOMP on it; twist your foot to the right, the left and back again. Now stoop down look at that smashed plant and get to digging. Write the first page, register for the class, talk to your mentor and take the first step. My dear, your garden has begun to grow – AGAIN!

CHAPTER 3:

WHAT TYPE OF SOUL-SOIL ARE YOU USING.

When I bought my house a few years ago, there was a spot in the backyard where the grass was trying to grow, but just couldn't get completely through. There was a layer of broken concrete left as evidence of something having occupied the 10 x 10 space near the fence. The first year I was there, I didn't mess with it, I just kept looking at it and wondering what had been there. The next year it became a flat-out eyesore and I wanted it gone. I asked my neighbor, what used to be there and he informed me a swing set had been built for the children who used to attend the former daycare.

Okay, concrete, it's heavy, how do I get rid of all this concrete? My grandfather was a brick mason by trade and I knew manual labor with brick and mortar was going to be some heavy duty physical work. I had a few contractors come to give some estimates for the removal, but their prices and my budget couldn't reach an agreement. So, I had to come up with an effective plan to take on a slab of concrete all by myself.

One of the contractors shared with me that it's best to do any yard work when the soil is wet. The very next rain,

I went for it. I remembered a scene from a movie where the landscaper used an iron rod to dig out a concrete pool. I found a broom handle in my garage and got to digging. To my delight and surprise, the slab was only about 1 ½ inches thick and as I dug into the soil, pulled the stick down and stepped on it, the first piece started giving way and then popped up. AAAwwww yeah, there was no stopping me now! It took me three hours to dig up the entire top layer. I remembered my grandfather teaching my brother, the best way to remove concrete is to break it into pieces. Every piece I dug up, I threw it on top of one of the many mounds I was building, in order to handle hauling it all away. I worked into sundown and by the time I was done the whole top slab was up. Through the dirt, I could still see rocks and pieces of concrete, so I had literally "only scratched the surface."

Next step, digging down into the soil, to get to the pieces down in the dirt that I couldn't see, but knew were there. I had to buy a metal shovel, so I would have more power to get below the surface soil. I kept digging and digging until I hit the concrete anchors that held the metal legs to keep the structure stationery. It took, four days, a bottle of Aleve, three bags of Epsom salt, a box of contractor bags, $60 and my niece's help to get all the concrete and metal out – whew!

Now, time to prepare the soil and put down seeds. I had to break up the dirt, add some fertilized potting soil for nutrients and lots of water before one seed could be dropped. I got a rake and spent hours, slowly and gently going back and forth through the soil, up and down and across to have the plot ready for seeding. This took a few more days of work, AFTER getting the concrete out.

And so it is, with the soil in the gardens of our hearts. Many of our hearts are hardened and covered with concrete layers of hate, pain, disappointment, unworthiness, abandonment, selfishness, insecurity and old wounds that are too thick to let anything or anyone in.

In Matthew 13, Jesus speaks of soil in rocky places where seeds can't grow. The seeds may grow out quickly, but when the sun comes out...

> *when the heat of a broken relationship cuts deep, when the pressure of a failure seems too hard to regroup, when something in life doesn't go as you planned or the unexpected takes a front seat...*

.... the seeds can't survive because they never took root in the soil that was too shallow.

We have different types of soil in our souls. Soil that allows us to blossom and flourish, be stagnant or die a slow spiritual death.   When we dig into our soul-soil, we need people and tools. Let's be real! If we were able to dig ourselves out of years of hurt, pain and a lack of forgiveness, how long would we remain in a state of hardness? We need to have sisters who will help us excavate with the shovels of openness and till with the spades of confession.

As women, we want to be happy, smile a lot and have many friends. We want to love and be loved, but life happens and instead of joy, we encounter pain over and over, and before we know it, the concrete wall of bitterness is there and how troubled we become when we have a hard heart. We live in a world of:

> *"smile and fake-it-till-you-make-it", because we don't want people to know about our pain.*

> *We don't want to be real and tell people we're disappointed that we didn't complete a goal.*

> *We don't want to let anyone know the sorrow of not having a child.*

We create a world of,

"you know I don't fool with people, I keep to myself and mind my own business,"

when on the inside, we are dying to have a conversation with our neighbor or sit in a coffee shop laughing with a friend over a latte'

We inhabit a world of shame because of the actions someone chose to take against us. We want to scream, hit and fight the person or people who hurt us and then made us suffer their shame.

We want to curse them out and ask them "WHY", why did you do this to me.

But instead, we suffer in silence and the concrete wall gets thicker and thicker year after year.

Take heart my sister, because all you need to tear that wall down into mounds that you can haul away, is within you. The Master Gardener has made all of us with soft, fertile soil in our souls. If you are reading this book right now, it's because the Creator wants you also to flourish and break free from the concrete that is holding your soul-soil captive.

Start small, write it down if you're not ready to talk with someone. Write one line a day.

"I am hurting,

I am in pain,

I am lonely,

I am disappointed,

I don't feel worthy,

Why did this happen to me?"

If tears and anger come with that one line, let them flow, don't hold them in, if your hand says keep writing – keep writing. As long as your hand and your heart say write, don't stop. Write until your fingers cramp up, write until the ink is wet with your tears – but write. This is how you begin to prepare your soul-soil for the seeds of a new life, seeds of a new attitude and thought process. The prophet Habakkuk says in 2:2 "Write down the revelation and make it plain….

Consult your source: Jesus, Buddha, Muhammad, Jehovah, or simply the Creator to lead you to the person who will begin to help you prepare your soul-soil for seeds. This may not be a counselor, a pastor or social worker. This may be your elderly neighbor who has lived a life filled with obstacles that she has had to overcome. This may be that lady you ride the bus with every day. Don't disregard the janitor at the school where you teach or the nursing assistant at the hospital where you work. It takes a second to say "Can I ask you a question – have you ever experienced such and so?" Now be prepared for the response, because what you will find is that all women have experienced so many of the same heart-aches and heart-breaks, only the names, faces, and places are different. And guess what, you'll see that she also needed to tell someone about her victory or how she's working towards her joy! Yes, my dear, it's going to be LOVELY!

None of us have been put on this earth to be alone. Even monks, after a temporary period of isolation, convene with their community. Making connections with other women can be so hard when we have been bruised and broken. Some of us want to voice what's wrong, but we simply can't find the words or the person to confide in.

"Trust" has become such a taboo word for those of us who have been deeply betrayed. We are now bitter and can't begin to open up to anyone to set ourselves free. Trusting someone to help you is not about them – it's about you. Who wants to continue living in a world imprisoned by the concrete slab that covers a heart that is stopping the enjoyment of life?

Your soul-soil is the beginning of your beautiful garden. A rose can't bloom, a daffodil can't blow in the wind and a pansy can't be tossed to and fro' by the rain without it having some roots planted in fertile soil.

Ask the Creator to lead you to the tools and women whom He knows will be able to help you overhaul your soul-soil. Softening your heart starts with you and your desire. It begins with you writing down your hurts and pains and then setting an intention to get help from another woman who was once, hard-hearted and is now healed.

CHAPTER 4:

WHAT BLESSINGS ARE MINE TO KEEP AND WHICH BLESSINGS ARE TO SHARE OR GIVE AWAY?

On a daily basis, throughout the day, we receive blessings from the Creator, mental, physical and spiritual blessings are among them. Some blessings are life lessons, that I affectionately refer to as "blessin' lessons", that we take with us and use for a life time. We share those lessons, and in different situations, we gain deeper insight and those lessons become invaluable.

Some blessings are for the moment. That card a friend surprises you with, just when you needed some encouragement. The bus coming just as you arrive at the bus stop and now you don't have to wait in the cold. That unexpected check you got in the mail just as you received an unexpected bill.

We receive blessings of knowledge, wisdom and maturity. Occurrences at work, school and everyday home life, teach us how to navigate through life's different "happenings". We learn to listen more and talk less. We are able to decipher what requires a response and what needs a simple nod of the head and that quiet "hhmmm."

As we pay attention to our lives throughout the day, we become our own witness to the miracles of daily blessings. When we are in-tune with the Creator, we receive blessings through different teachings, corrections, rebukes and encouragement.

As women, we are by nature "givers." Out of our own life-gardens, we give to our spouses, children, family, friends co-workers, and strangers, usually, without a second thought. We strategically plan how we're going to meet the needs of someone in or near our circle. We bring our regular cashier a baby shower gift because we notice she's pregnant. We give our co-worker a Walmart gift card after hearing she doesn't have any toiletries at home. We give, we give and we give.

Sometimes we give so much that our spirits are affected and our life gardens begin to feel out of balance in some way. Somewhere we can start feeling like "Whoa, I've given this and that and now I need something and I can't get a lick of help". We can become bitter and selective with whom and with what we give. How did this happen? It happens because we give without discernment.

"Why do I need discernment, I should just give."

Yes, we should give. Yes, we should sow into the universe; yes, we should give to our fellow man because it's one of our duties to humanity. Yes, we should share our blessings, because the bible says, "He who refreshes others, will himself be refreshed – Proverbs 27:17. But discernment teaches us what blessings we are to share, give away or keep for ourselves.

Do you know the woman who boasts or is known for "Giving the shirt off her back"? Yes, you know her, because you've been her, and I've been her. This is the woman who will give you her last dollar, share her meal with you, let you live in her house and use her car. This is the woman who gives her signature to co-sign for a car or signs her name on a payday loan for a friend to buy her children Christmas gifts. She is the woman who gives and gives and learns through one or more of those experiences that giving without discernment is very unwise giving.

There are plants of blessings in our gardens that we are to share and flowers that we are to keep and enjoy for ourselves. If we give a rose away here and a flower away there when our gardens are empty, it is not because people came and plundered them; it is because we gave until the gardens were depleted.

Discernment teaches us that we can enjoy our abundant, flourishing garden, we can walk through the garden of our lives and enjoy the smell of success and touch the rose petal of hard work. It is OK for us to look at the garden and smile at what we've labored to build. It is alright to gaze at the beauty of the garden you've worked, tended, tilled and watered and now has a mind-altering aroma of success and envelopes all who come into your presence, with majestic beauty.

The garden of your life has been worked at and worked out. You have dealt with and been healed from your pain! You've confronted your past and stopped it from drowning your present and killing your future! You did bounce back from that divorce! You're almost through the years of a rebellious teenager! You have finally forgiven your molester! Daily you overcome the voices that say "you are not worthy!" Oh, yes, my Queen, you have put work in this garden - for YOU to enjoy, not to just give away. When I want to give, and have counted a cost that would be too great, I have a talk with myself and say:

"Self, all that has grown over the fence, out of your abundance, the crowds are welcome to it and can have it, but what's inside this here garden, is YOURS, MINE and OURS"

Let me be clear. There will be times that sacrificial giving is necessary and you may have to share a meal with a neighbor so both families can eat. I want to make sure we understand the importance of counting the cost when giving.

I didn't get this until WELL into my adulthood after many hard knocks against my head. If I give you the shirt off my back – then I'm going to be cold. But if I teach you how to get your own shirt-and keep it, then we both can teach two more women, who will teach two more and everyone will have and keep a shirt.

This wisdom was earned after years of letting people live with me and my children. I put cars in my name that were in accidents and I had to go to court– alone. This understanding grew after years of loaning money that was never repaid. Doing financial favors for people, only to find out, they had no plans of returning the favor – they just didn't tell me.

I have learned that when a person has not taken the time or made the effort to tend to something in their own garden, they are surely not going to have any concern about something going wrong in yours – Bridgett McGill

We learn through much trial and error that it's okay to say "No". What we have to learn on a deeper level is to say

"No" and that it's "OKAY". I remember when I first started building my tool box. My grandfather would say

"Baby, don't let people use your tools, they don't give 'em back and when you ask for your tools back, they get mad."

My grandfather had truly spoken a prophetic word, as I found this to be true in loaning as well as giving. Although giving and loaning are two different things, counting the cost is equally important for both. Do you remember a time of offering to help someone because you saw their need, only to have them respond later with the ungrateful?

I didn't ask you for help, you offered.

Have you ever loaned someone something and then when you ask for it, the response was:

"you too petty"

"Imma give you that lil 20 dollars back, dang"

"man, you still calling me about them lil ran over shoes."

HA, I know some of you are screaming "YES" right now, because it is the nature of the beast called humanity. But all is not lost, because in these situations, we learn the value of our life- gardens. We learn to keep our umbrellas, so when it rains, we don't get wet. We are okay with the party not being held at our house, because at the last party, something was broken and no one wanted to pay for it. We appreciate the beauty in the gardens of our lives, because gardens don't just become beautiful, we work at making our lives something to behold.

We have to train ourselves to love our gardens EVERY DAY through self-care and self-love. We finally get it, that our life garden is worthy of beauty and deserving of abundant life pleasures. There will always be people in situations who believe they are entitled to the flowers in our gardens, or they want to steal our plants of joy, but discernment is not only our friend; it is also our protector.

We have the power to decide what to give away and what to keep. So, enjoy your garden sister and be happy with the beautiful, fragrant, life-garden the Creator has designed just for you.

CHAPTER 5:

HOW MANY GARDENS CAN YOU GROW AT ONCE?

In this busy thing, we call life, we have assigned daily duties. As wives, we tend to our husbands, tilling their God-given needs for love and respect. As mothers, we take care of our children – sowing seeds of security and empowerment, cooking, homework, bed time stories, basketball practice, and Sunday preparations for the week to come. As entrepreneurs or employees, we give to our business or workplace through time, preparation, coming early, staying late, meetings and events.

All in all, we are busy with much to do. Most of the time we are so occupied tending to the gardens around us, that we forget about our own life-gardens. You're leaning over the fence with the right hand in the garden of your adult child. Now, with the left hand, you lean over and reach in the garden of your family member older than you. Bending backwards, with hand over your head, reach in the garden of your next-door neighbor. GEESH, how tiring it is tending to everyone's garden, and right before our eyes, our gardens become dry, patchy, dull and unmoving.

We become multi-faceted through relationships of all kinds, old habits, new ideas, generational curses and family traits. We get overloaded with everybody's issues and problems and add them to our already full, busting at the seams garden. Can't you picture it vividly, the white picket fence around your garden, with cracked slats and hinges about to burst? With one small push of another problem or situation, our garden will sscrreeaaammmm!!!!!!!!

A skill we must master is keeping our lives free of people and things that have no business occupying space in our lives because they or it is not serving a useful purpose or adding to our growth. We must protect our precious garden space and be alert to the subtle creeping in, that happens through our sentimentality, lack of discernment, being overly emotional or simply not paying attention.

It's always too late when we wake up and ask ourselves:

what happened to my life?

Why am I feeling this way, stuck and can't move?

Who am I now, where did I go, how did I lose myself?"

We often become bitter, depressed or both about having taken care of everyone else's garden, while our own go un-attended – through no one's fault but our own. We begin to desire the things that used to give us identity or made us feel alive. We want the focus back on us, so we revisit gardens where we used to live - gardens of comfort and familiarity.

You know the gardens I'm speaking of – past relationships, bad habits, double life. We have to be very cautious of the beckoning of our former gardens, where we used to dwell when we were straddling the fence. We made the decision to jump down on one side or the other, but when we get lost in our everyday lives, we take a step here and a step there toward that forbidden fence.

Be careful of that one finger touching that "back in the day" spot on the fence, in a blink, our entire hand is up there, and our temptations are pulling the rest of our body up by the bootstraps and now we're riding cowboy, trying to figure out how we got up there and what is it going to take to get down – and stay down – for good!

The key is balance! We are responsible for tending our children's gardens. We teach them how to live, love and be responsible. If we are married, we have a garden within a garden. You have to maintain your own garden, because you are still your own being. However, the bible says the two become one. Therefore, that garden within in your garden must be tended with diligence.

Balance is a small word, with a big meaning. We have to make room for ourselves and ask ourselves daily:

Do I feel taken care of?

It's okay to ask your husband for some time to rest so you can take care of you; stop being Wonder Woman. Newsflash: she's not real. The kids will be okay if you take one day to sit and watch tv by yourself, or go to the park without them. Make sure you get up early one or two days a week to do some deep breathing, take a hot bath and lather your entire body with oil.

Don't let yourself forget what it feels like to dress up and go out. Do you own at least one set of matching bra and panties? Is there a pair of thigh-hi stockings lurking in the back of your drawer waiting to be pulled seductively up your legs when you need an ego boost? There will always be a garden that needs tending, but make sure your garden is taken care of first. When your garden is not well nourished, you will give out of your lack, rather than your abundance and that my dear, is not true giving.

CHAPTER 6:

THE BEAUTIFUL GARDEN OF PLASTIC AND STONE.

Have you ever been in a store that sells beautiful home décor? Quality centerpieces with flowers that look so real you can't help but to touch them. The petals never droop, nor is the soil ever in need of water or fertilizer – PERFECT ALWAYS! Just like our sister that dwells in the garden of plastic and stone – always perfect.

Who of us knows this woman – Ms. Perfection? With I's dotted and T's crossed, not a hair out of place, language articulate, car detailed, home impeccable. She never cries or shows emotion, because she wouldn't dare give anyone a chance to say she broke down in public. When she speaks - she's direct, choosing when to laugh because most things to her are foolishness. In all her perfection, she must be EXHAUSTED!

This is the life of a woman whose garden is so beautiful to the eye, but on careful examination, something seems off and all is not as it appears.

This is the woman bruised and beaten, hurt, abandoned and betrayed, scars, seen and unseen. She has an invisible wall that moves through the garden so that every flower touched, has no feeling, every plant spoken to can't respond. She won't allow herself to be hurt ever again.

She is self-sufficient and overly independent. She doesn't let anyone help her with anything because her mind tells her:

Nothing is free, it may not cost you now, but it will cost you later

She makes sure to "control" E-V-E-R-Y-T-H-I-N-G!

She does not allow herself to be blessed because she thinks

this is not a real blessing, this person is gonna want something in return

She wears a mask that speaks "I have it alllllll together", but behind the mask, her face is moist with tears. She doesn't have or know the value of great relationships because of past betrayals – she does not trust – anyone!

She simply walks through her garden of plastic and stone, dusting and wiping, making sure that everything in her garden is "PERFECT."

Psalm 119:96 - To all perfection I see a limit, but your commands are boundless.

If our dear sister reads this passage and took it to heart, she will be able to EXHALE! This woman is ready to scream and let it all go.

She wants to love and trust, she desires to walk through her garden and dismantle the pseudo altars and kick the vases and flower pots over – just so she can feel something – anything.

She wants to love and be loved. She desires to water her garden with real tears, so real flowers can grow. There is a deep longing to tell someone about the hurt and pain so she can forgive and be set free of the hatred that's wedged between her heart muscles. She desperately needs to laugh until she wets her pants. Her body wants to cry until her throat is dry. She wishes so much that she could sit with a group of women and be real for once – talk freely, openly not caring what comes out. She wants to live and be ALIVE!

She wants her garden to be beautiful – authentic – drooping when it needs water and standing at attention to the morning sun. She's worn out from maintaining the garden of perfection, that is always beautifully – unchanged!

If only she could sit in the dirt of her garden and start digging in and pulling out. She wants to till the soil and dig deep into the roots – BUT WAIT – there are no roots, because the only thing she's rooted in is her PERFECTION!

Then it happens, one day as she's frantically dusting and wiping, trying to keep it altogether, the porcelain vase full of old pain and deep hurts begins to wobble. It shakes and she tries to catch it but it's too late – CRASH! It hits the dirt and shatters into hundreds of pieces. She looks down and does her usual strategic assessment to solve a problem. She bends down to pick up the pieces in a hurry before her brokenness is detected and someone sees that she's shattered. In her haste, she picks up a piece of the porcelain that digs deep into the flesh of her finger; the cut is deep. She can't stop the bleeding with the finger to lip pressure; the blood is now flowing freely.

With every droplet that splashes in the dirt, cracks in her perfect wall begin to give way. She doesn't try to stop the tears that are caressing the shape of her cheeks and flowing down to her neck and chest. With each moan, there is a gasp like choking, then screams. She screams at who hurt her, she hollers at the one who abandoned her, and she curses everyone who pretended to love her. She asks why of everyone who didn't listen to her cries for help.

She is now on her knees, muddied from the tear soaked dirt. Her nails are dirty from digging into the mud. The blood is now clotted, she crawls to a plastic fern, she digs and digs until it's plastic roots are visible and she throws it over the fence.

She remembers the words of the Master Gardener and runs to the shed in the corner of the garden. She had tried to open the shed in years past, but had never heeded to the instructions:

Caution: CAN ONLY BE OPENED WITH DIRTY HANDS!

She stands there, hands shaking, wondering if now, right now, she can finally open the doors and access the seeds of new life, fertilizer of forgiveness, rakes, spades and pruning shears of change and transformation.

She turns the handle and the door opens. The tears began to flow again as she touches the burlap sack of seeds, she buries her fingers into the bag. Having been so used to the feel of plastic and stone, the prickly texture of the bag makes her heart race.

She grabs the seeds, a spade and fills a pitcher with water. She runs back to the hole left by the plastic fern. Carefully planting the seed and covering it with dirt, she pours water on her new life and sits back in the dirt. She thanks God for the dirt on her hands, she thanks Him for the tears, the yells, the screams. She looks again at the small mound and realizes, her entire garden could be new and deeply rooted, one plant at a time. At that moment, she inhales deeply and breathes out "YES!"

Are you this woman? Do you need to talk to someone, write a letter to another? Are there bottled up tears that need to be unleashed so the pain can flow from your body? Today, is the day my sister, to get dirty in your pain, sit with it. It is the season to become real and truthful with yourself. It doesn't matter who listens and who doesn't, no more facades. Give yourself permission to snatch that band-aid of pretending off, feel the hurt and let that open wound heal with the air of relief. Pick up a sorrow filled vase, throw it down and kick the pieces with a smile.

This season is not for the person who hurt you, this season is for you! It will take some time to dig up each plant, but flower by flower, your garden of plastic and stone can become beautiful, authentic and real.

CHAPTER 7:

THE WOMAN IN THE GARDEN OF SELFISHNESS.

This woman's garden is full and fruitful; she has worked hard to keep it ALL to herself. Never stopping to prune a plant hitting her in the face or making room in the soil for her plants to grow and expand, she overlooks the garden's full potential, because she is simply – unwilling to let go.

So selfish, she would rather look at roots protruding through the dirt and let them grow above the soil before she would give away something she has worked so hard to possess. It never crosses her mind to divide the plants and repot them to leave outside the gate to share with others. Giving something that she has earned to someone is UNHEARD OF. So, there she is in her garden, thick and lush. She cannot sit, walk or move, because the garden is so bountiful and full, she can only stand; she is stuck and unable to grow. Have you ever heard the saying:

In the space where nothing can get out, neither can anything get in?

Dictionary.com defines selfish as an adjective that means lacking consideration for others, concerned chiefly with one's own personal profit or pleasure.

How does a woman become selfish, what happened in her life that made her this way? Is it an intentional selfishness, or did it develop without her even recognizing this flaw is now a part of who she is? There are many roads that can lead to a heart of SELFISHNESS; let's walk along a few of them.

She was the only child or youngest child who never had to share anything simply because there was no one to share it with. She grew up having everything at her disposal, all to herself, so her mind believes this is the way it's always been, so this is the way it should always be.

She may come from the big family where she had to share EVERYTHING. She wore hand-me-downs from her big sister, or swapped clothes and shoes with the little sister. She had to sleep with her sister and eat with her brothers. When she was able to have anything to herself, there would be no more sharing involved.

Is she the woman who grew up with nothing? Raised by the grandmother who provided the basics: food, clothes, shelter, nothing more, nothing less. She has a fear of not having, because there was always so little. That fear keeps her from letting anything go. She has every pair of shoes she ever bought and dresses that are 10 years out of style. She is determined to never know "lack" again. She's not going to chip in on the gas because you're going to the same place. No matter how many people are at the table she's going to have the waiter charge her card, for her meal only.

How about our beloved sister who has finally arrived? She and SECOND place are on a first name basis. She's always been second choice, second rate, always working hard, but still in second place. When she slides into that first-place positon, she never stops running and never looks back. The dread of ever going back to second place keeps her focused, looking forward. She pays no attention to the sister on the right or the left, because if she helps them, she might get weak somehow and lose her first-place spot.

> "Reach back and help you, I had to work to get here – NOT!"

Selfish woman numero uno! She has never lacked anything and has always had an abundance; she is just greedy and wants it all to herself, not wanting anyone around to have even a little. The hardness of her heart makes her so close to evil it's scary.

All of these women are in great need of a mended garden. They have to prepare for battle to work at trimming their abundance and blessing others with their overflow. They need a machete to cut off the branches of "all mine". It's going to take a hacksaw to get through the vines of greed that have entangled them.

A hand suddenly appears, combing through the brush for help, our sister wants to be rescued. The Master Gardener hears her cry for help and sees her outstretched hand. She is ready to be free of the plenty that is suffocating her. As any good father would do, he sends his daughter help. There are sisters who have been sitting on benches outside her garden awaiting instruction. They stand, take a deep breath, pick up their tools and go in.

Some are pricked by her harshness, others are cut by her short temper. One sister is exhausted because she's working doubly hard. Sister selfish looks at every bushel about to leave the garden and yells,

"I need to keep that!"
"Sister haul away" says "No you don't, let go"

and pries the basket from her hand, disregarding her angry stares.

They work diligently, weeks at a time teaching her how to purge, prune and trim. The team encourages her to smile as she gives away plants. They comfort her as she stubbornly puts flowers in decorated vases and lines them against the fence for others to take and enjoy. Her skipping through the garden is evidence of the space that has been cleared. She is enjoying the laughter and company of the workers who started as friends and are now her sisters. She OVERstands that she was denying herself, by holding on so tightly and now smiles at having her garden in full view.

She greets her neighbors with a smile; they wave and say "thank you" for the plants and flowers that are now in their gardens, that are gifts from her once overstuffed landscape. She has given and been given to. She has received understanding and knows that with everything she has given away, she has gained twice as much. She has become delighted in her garden because now she can breathe and grow.

CHAPTER 8:

THE LEAVES OF GRACE AND MERCY.

My friend Yolanda has lots of experience with gardens. Every spring her father plants a yard filled with cabbage, yellow peppers, bell peppers, cucumbers, tomatoes, corn, green onions, string beans, mustard and turnip greens. She told me that her father uses the fall leaves he rakes up as a protective covering atop his garden during the fall and winter seasons. Another friend added the leaves keep the plants from moving and shifting during the rainy season. I immediately thought of God as this kind of protector over my life-garden when I'm not in a due season.

When we are in seasons of growth, we are on the mountain top of spirituality doing our holy dance before the Lord.

Lord if you come today, I can make it!

We can be in a spiritually sound place - life is good and all is truly well. We can easily discern situations and give spiritual advice downloaded directly to us from the Holy Spirit. Satan will shoot arrows that bounce off our impenetrable walls of holiness.

But what happens when we are not dancing and twirling about happily at the mountain's peak? There are seasons in our lives when we will not be glowing and growing, but learning and changing, and those times are not always easy, in fact, they can be downright rough and tough.

What's going on when we are sitting in the valley in a season of darkness, transformation or sin? What if we need to build spiritual muscles in a weak area or revisit a space where we need to gain deeper convictions?

While we are in the valley, we are protected by the leaves of the Holy spirit that keep us in place in the Lord. We don't know what's going on in the world above the soil nor should we dwell on getting back to the mountain top. Let's not whine and ask, why am I here Lord, in the dark? I was doing good, I obey you God, I love you. Why do I have to go down into the valley now?

Instead of focusing on going back up top, sit in the valley and see the purpose in the process. While you're in the valley – ask the Creator:

What should I be learning while I'm here Lord?

What is my lesson?

What do you want to teach me?

What do you want to show me?

What do you want me to understand?

Are there relationships that need mending, do you have behaviors or characteristics that need to be dealt with and adjusted? What situations have you kept coming back to because the lesson hasn't been learned?

What is your mindset while in the valley? Do you still see the Creator or do you think He abandoned you to figure it on your own, while He sits at the mountain top waiting for you to ascend? Do you trust that the Father is still with you, right there in the muck and mire? Are you in the valley because it's your planting time or are you there because you took yourself there?

Walk with me to get a clear picture of what "taking yourself to the valley" looks like. At the writing of this book, I've been in my chosen faith for 24 years. I spent nine of those years living a double life. I went to bible study every Tuesday and attended service faithfully every Sunday, sometimes leaving my boyfriend in my bed, or having just left his. I didn't go back to my old habits of cursing and smoking, and for the most part I still "appeared" to be walking the "Christian" walk.

I allowed people into my world who I knew wouldn't question my ungodly relationships. There were no discussions about my "boyfriends" because they didn't see anything wrong with the way I was living. They couldn't call me to any scriptures, nor could I them, because we were all living the same way.

I still loved the Lord, and I didn't participate in any egregious activities. I had boyfriends who I was immoral with, and DAILY I walked the walk of hypocrisy. I chose the parts of the bible I wanted to follow and paid no attention to the verses that spoke to my disobedient life-style.

I was strategic in my mess. My friends who knew the Word and would surely ask questions or take me to the "ignored" scriptures, were kept outside that part of my world.

I cried myself to sleep many nights, because the hypocrisy of my life was so heavy. More times than not, I wasn't enjoying the sex and despised those relationships because they were temporary substitutes and a constant reminder of the man I really wanted from God but He was taking wwwwaayyyy too long to deliver for my patience. During this dark time, I knew that I had dragged myself to the valley and was keenly aware that I was holding myself hostage in deep despair of my own free will. I was on the lukewarm fence between hot for the Lord and cold for the love of my sin.

"BUT GOD", as cliché' as it sounds, the leaves of God's mercy covered me. The leaves of grace kept me in his arms when I was living contrary to His word. He was keeping me when I didn't want to be kept. His Grace, ahhhh his grace. In those nine years, neither I or my children were ever hurt, beaten or abused; we were truly spared. We often see headlines of girls beaten, raped and in some cases murdered by their mother's boyfriends.

This double life didn't come without a price. I paid heavy wages emotionally, spiritually, and financially. We are often deceived by suffering when it's not physical, but mental, emotional and financial suffering are just as damaging. As mentioned in a previous chapter, I did a "favor" for one boyfriend by putting his car title in my name; that resulted in my getting stuck with $2000 worth of parking tickets. Another car was totaled after being driven into a steel beam, because that boyfriend was drinking and driving. I loaned another one $1000 to get out of jail. Even after he paid the debt, he felt I was wrong for making him repay the money because we were a "team". My choices in men were a direct result of me focusing on what I wanted "a man" instead of waiting on the Lord to bless me with what I deserved. When living in darkness, we cannot see the beauty of our own light. Depression and anger kept growing!

But Jehovah-Jireh was and still is my Deliverer. In 2013, The Lord made it clear to me just how much I had taken his mercy and grace for granted and said in no uncertain terms, in a very quiet whisper,

"you need to make a decision about your life, but you will get off this fence. You are going to make a choice to jump down on one side or the other, or I'm going to make it for you. You will no longer live in mockery of the cross and live your life in vain using my name. You have to decide if you are all in or all out, there is no in-between.

I cried out to God, "I wanna change Father, but I don't know how, please help me", and the Lord sent my friend and sister in Christ Daisy, to help save me from myself. I had known the roots of many of my mindsets and behaviors and was aware of the generational curses that were on me. I compare it to standing at a well, where I knew there was fresh water, but I didn't know how to operate the pump to get the water out. Over a period of 14 weeks, I met with Daisy and went through spiritual life coaching. It was the best money I ever invested in myself. The rest is history and this book is part of my testimony of deliverance and repairing all the damage I had caused to my life garden and the gardens of my children. This book was my assignment and I had to dwell, learn, and repent in the valley to come out on the other side for it to be completed.

We are not always in the valley due to sin just because our gardens are out of season. When we're in the valley, the Creator has not abandoned us; in fact, he has gently led us to the valley and is sitting in the next seat. In the darkness, He is there, in the mud, He is there. When there is darkness, we cannot see, so we have no choice but to listen to his voice. Some days you have to dig in deep, wrestle and fight. Other days you have to just sit, and be still and know that he is God (Psalm 46:10).

As those spiritual muscles become stronger, relationships are mended; you've learned to talk less and listen more, because you realize the battle is the Lords' all the time. You cried, yelled, screamed and cried some more, you've made your way through the season in victory. The leaves of protection have dissolved into your garden and become food that sustain you the entire winter. As you emerge, you have grown stronger and into the vibrant sun of new beginnings, you are overjoyed as you realize, the Creator surely brought you through.

It's important to journal during your seasons of rest so you can go back and reflect on all that you have learned. This helps you get through the next season to remind you that the valley is not a bad place, but a necessary time in space to get you to the next level.

Don't be afraid to seek the help you need. Ask the Father for direction and prepare yourself for the answer. He is preparing you for an assignment and ensuring you are ready to complete the assignment and get an "A"!

CHAPTER 9:

THE GARDEN OF COMPLACENCY.

Give a man a fish and he eats for a day – teach a man to fish and he eats for a lifetime.   Chinese Proverb.

The same is true for the woman next to you, who instead of tending to her own garden, constantly imposes on yours. Why? Because she is not making an effort to make her garden beautiful. She looks at you and says "It doesn't take all that" "You don't have to make all that sacrifice, or put all that work in – EVERYDAY!" But when she's alone, she gazes at the garden of her life and ponders at the same four or five roses that grow back every year, the perennials that come back to the same place near the gate each spring. She wonders why the ivy vine never grows beyond knee high on the gate.

She is content with her "do-just-enough-to-get-by" life-garden.
"Well, at least it's not all brown and completely empty".

But what else is it not? It's not watered, tilled or pruned. You come to this garden every day and you're okay with how it looks – your garden of complacency. This woman is not suffering in her life; she's not in any pain or dealing with any grief, but she's not working to be the best HER that she can be.

"Those brown patches aren't that bad, nobody can even see them, over in the corner by the gate – I'm okay".
"What about the green patches, don't they count for something?"

Yes, they do, because what we do well, we keep doing that, what we don't do so well, we ignore. But how long my sister, are you going to keep existing instead of actually living?

Teaching a woman how to tend to and maintain her own life garden is beneficial for you and her. It takes discernment, wisdom and patience. If she's ready to listen and grow, pick up your spades and shovels of love and encouragement and dig in. If she's not, plant the seeds and meet her where she is.

When a woman is content in her life of complacency -which we all have been at one time or another - she may not be ready to do the work. She will be just fine sharing and reaping the benefits of yours. If she's ready, teach her how to take care of her own garden in or out of season. She may not want to listen at first and you don't need to press the issue, but what you will have to do is take a stand. Stand firm and let her know she will no longer be able to come and partake of the fruits of your labor. This woman is usually close to you, that's why she's so comfortable imposing. She has a job, but always needs to borrow money. She always needs some place to stay, because she lacks the discipline to create a budget that would allow her to move into or remain in her own apartment. Instead she shops and spends frivolously. She has a place to live, but never has food or household supplies. She may grocery shop, but loves to sit at your table instead of cooking. Don't be angry with her; she's always lived this way and no one has challenged her to live differently. In her mind, this is all-right. She believes it is better for people to give than to receive – to her. She knows that you have an abundance, why should she not enjoy your overflow?

Let's take a deeper look at our sister. She admires the lush beauty of your garden and enjoys leaning over the fence and being intoxicated with the smell of your exquisite roses. Her daily visits to your garden are the highlight of her day. The love of your rich and fertile soil is evident as she walks through bare-footed and carefree. Her feet dance as she skips and laughs freely.

The moment you take a stand and force her to leave, the pout on her face is priceless when you inform her that playtime is over. Your index finger directs her to the gate, with instructions to pick up her shoes on the way out.

She moseys back to her garden swinging shoes in hand and thoughts of exhaustion cloud her mind. She is frustrated with the mere thought of how to get her garden to flourish, not to emulate yours, but flourishing for herself. Her garden is not all lost, but does need some work. Her life shows signs of promise, with several patches of green grass mixed in with some brown spots. There are a few roses, an overgrown hosta and returning pansies along the fence that make their annual appearance, indicating that there is some good soil there.

She wants to dismiss the thoughts of hard work with her repetitive statement: "It just doesn't take all that!" She has slowed in the walk towards her garden and is about to make the turn to the entry gate. She tries to calculate just how much work it will take to get her garden to the next level.

Her mind drifts back to the sweat and toil she sees her neighbor exert at the beginning of every planting season. The neighbor's garden does not start out lush, but by mid-spring her neighbor is relaxing and waiting for the blooming to begin.

She watches her lug in bag after bag of potting soil, new pots, decorated fences and lattice. Her nose and top lip curl up remembering the stinky manure. The gardener spends one full day hauling one wheel barrel after another of the smelly fertilizer to cover the full garden after she has prepared the soil. She rakes and spreads all day until the entire garden is covered.

She rests for a few days and waits for the rain. She takes of her shoes and walks back and forth through the garden in what seems to be an effort to cover every inch with her feet.

The woman in the garden of complacency often thought about the condition and smell of her neighbor's feet and legs after a day of walking through her manure laden garden. The stinky smell wafts through the neighborhood for a couple of weeks with every wind that blows reminding every one of her hard work. We all have manure in our lives that can be used to fertilize our gardens, our recognition and use of the manure is determined by us individually.

Then the garden's magic happens; the plot of earth where there was once dirt is now wonderful to the eyes. Greens, reds and yellows, so vibrant, they blind you under the sun's light. The aromas so provocative, make you stop, close your eyes and inhale deeply as you take it all in. Now what is her neighbor doing? She's filling vases of love to give as "thank yous" to those who taught her to work hard in her life-garden. She creates arrangements of encouragement for those she wants to inspire to do the same. She doesn't worry when the hard rains come, because all of her plants and flowers are deeply rooted. When the rain settles, everything stands again at attention to their friend, the Sun.

Coming back into reality, our complacent sister turns the corner, peers into her life and just as she reaches the gate to her garden, she smiles at her decision.

"Yes, tomorrow I will go to the Master Gardener, humbly, with pen and pad, sit at her feet and learn – how to make my garden grow"

CHAPTER 10:

THE GARDEN OF ABUNDANCE

Lush, vibrant, thick, rich colors, exhilarating smells, textures and aromas that tease all five senses, full and luscious with room to grow, are beautiful to behold.

This if a life-garden so peaceful we can sit with our eyes closed, legs crossed, inhaling and exhaling deeply. This is the life of a gardener full of rest, peace, conviction and stability. This woman can sit and enjoy her garden because she has sweat, toiled, labored, cried, danced and surrendered to the Creator and followed his instructions.

She is protective of her garden and uses discernment with all who desire to enter. When you look into this woman's garden; the serenity mesmerizes you. As you observe her reading books and acknowledging every passer-by with a smile and a wave, you are enchanted.

The calmness in her garden is eerie to those who are restless, yet intriguing to those seeking solace in their own gardens.

To those who inquire how her serenity was obtained, she asks specific questions, before they are invited in to learn what the Master Gardener has taught her. She makes sure she will not be casting her pearls to swine.

As the guests arrive, they agree to be in complete humility to accept the teaching, no matter how hard or intense. No matter how deep they have to dig or how many buckets of water need to be drawn; they must fully commit to the journey.

How is this woman able to teach sisters to plant and grow successfully? She's lived in every other garden, and so have you and I.

At different times, in our lives we will experience each garden explored throughout the pages of this book, because that's the roller coaster of life. We have to decide every day, the level of beauty we desire in our gardens.

Our life-gardens can bless or curse. We have the power to give and speak life into others. Do we allow our gardens to be blessed? As we desire to give life and nourish others, do we allow ourselves to be nourished and gifted to in return? When someone comes to the garden gate with a gift, do we refuse it, because we believe we have enough?

When we allow our gardens to receive, we make room for our gardens to flourish even more. We create space for plants of love and inspiration to be imparted to us.

Women have such amazing feminine power. We have within us the power to birth nations, divide armies and incite wars. We can build our men up with quiet loyalty or tear him down with the simplest of words.

We can impact our children and create a band of angels or a den of demons. This is our garden – our lives. Our gardens don't just serve to bless, provide and comfort us, but also others. When someone comes into our gardens, there should be a peace and serenity that is peculiar and welcoming; touching all who enter, with gentleness and patience

Our life-gardens touch people in this way, if this is the state of our gardens.

We will experience change and transformation as our gardens go through different seasons. We may have to change our tools or replenish the soil with nutrients. When situations move us to change, we must adjust, and as women, we are brilliant at adapting.

We learn to make a way out of no way and take a patch of earth and turn it into a plot of beauty.

All women have the capacity to impart special gifts to every person they meet, no matter how brief the encounter.

Time and situations can affect our garden's make-up, but not it's God given intention. Life is going to happen every day and that - we cannot change. Each sunrise brings with it the question,

What does my garden need today, sun, cultivation, fertilizer water or rest?

Every day, with joy, each of us must look in the mirror and ask ourselves the question,

How does my garden grow?

ACKNOWLEDGMENTS:

To The Most High God, your favor has blessed and transformed my life. Thank you for being a Lord that is up close and personal, showing me your love, that I have never had to question.

*

To my siblings, David, Kenyatta and Chynel – Thank you for teaching me a true leader is first, a true servant. The Most High knew we would be a great team. We Still Winning!

*

To ALL my girls, too many to name, I am FAVORED by The Most High to have you all as my friends. Thank you for your input and encouragement to finish this book.

*

To my cousin Khaleelah – your infectious laughter has sent me to the bathroom on too many occasions. I thank you for your continuous encouragement, it has impacted me more than you will ever know.

*

Barbara Henry – My writing mentor, editor and friend. Thanks for always believing in me and praying for me. Thank you for always encouraging me and for the hours you spent with me bringing this project to completion. You are a true blessing.